Woman to Woman:
Powerful Affirmations

Foreword by Sherri J

FULL DISCLAIMER

The material in this book may include information by third parties. Third-party affirmations comprised of the opinion expressed by their owners. As such, the author of this book does not assume responsibility for any third-party affirmations.

The publishing of such third-party affirmations do not constitute the author's guarantee of any information or instruction contained within the third-party affirmation. Publication of such third-party affirmatios is simply a expression of the author's own opinion of that material.

Any questions or comments regarding the Disclaimer for Woman to Womon: Powerful Affirmations please contact info@woman2womanbook.com.

Contents

Self- affirmation encourages you to think positively about the important things in your life.

In today's society, we are consistently overwhelmed and inundated with media that are designed to capture our attention. We have access to multiple social media platforms, innumerable places from which to stream movies, live television and music, and technological devices that are intuitive. Our thought-life becomes encapsulated with the posting of our friends and follows; our minds receive subconscious suggestions about what we should wear, where we should eat and where we should travel. Before we know it, we find ourselves comparing our lives and entire existence with 15 seconds of someone else's. It becomes so easy to get caught up in everything and everyone competing for our attention and our focus that it becomes easy to forget life's top priority—the nurturing and care for self.

Believe it or not, often times, we don't even realize that we are meditating upon—and therefore, affirming—negative things about ourselves. For example, when we find ourselves in moments of frustration, we may think about what is frustrating us, how we've allowed ourselves to get into this particular situation, what we should've done or what we could've done. We subconsciously begin to play over and over again in our minds those things that are not good for us; therefore, we may see the negative result manifest in our lives. Through the affirmation of that which is good, that which is powerful, and that which is loving about ourselves, we begin to condition our minds to revert to those affirmations of positivity.In those moments of negativity, these affirmations bring us back to our center so that we can redirect our energy in a positive and productive way and handle it!

Affirmation is the action of declaring something into existence. It is a form of prayer, meditation or auto-suggestion, declaring that which your heart desires. Affirmation is a partnership of what you truly think and how you truly feel about what you want to see in your life. You see, to simply repeat the affirmation is not enough to make your dreams manifest. You have to FEEL like you are already experiencing the life that you want. Your heart and your head must be on one accord. If you do not have feelings of positivity and love attached to the thought that you are affirming and thus, speaking, you are slowing down the process by which you will see that thing happen in your life. Think about it this way, every thought that we have and every feeling we experience sends a message out to the Universe. In turn, the Universe interprets our thoughts and our feelings and gives us back exactly what we asked for in those thoughts and feelings. So you ask, "How can I ensure that the Universe gives me exactly what I want?" Well, it is through the intentionality of thought and the redirection of any feeling or emotion that is not positive.

In pursuing the life of your dreams, it's important to affirm that which you want. You'll attract that which you affirm daily and focus on consistently. Therefore, focus on what you want and not what you don't want. For example, if there is a particular business you wish to start, focus on that exact business. Think about the specific experiences you will want to offer to your customer or client base; think about the kinds of experiences you will have managing your business; imagine yourself easily able to complete payroll and provide monetary incentives for your employees; picture yourself exceeding your sales or profit goals. The more you set your focus, with intention, using self-affirmations, the more you will see the true desire of your heart materialize. Wherever your focus lies in your mind, your eyes will see that in your reality. It is paramount to be intentional about that upon which you focus and harness the power of affirmation, even in those moments you aren't feeling your best.

Over the course of my journey in entrepreneurship, outside of my work ethic, preparation, and sheer determination to succeed, self- affirmation has been the key, unlocking doors to each and every new level of growth, both personally and professionally, that I have attained. I am undoubtedly the woman I am today because of the unyielding focus upon my goals through self-affirmation. It is my hope, as you embark upon this journey of affirming those things about which you are most passionate, that you begin to see your life change in ways more beautiful than you could've ever imagined. So, remember; think it, feel it, and speak it until you see it and don't forget to collect some souvenirs of your success along the way.

Dedication:
I dedicate this book to my best friend, Neda.
Thank you for always encouraging me and
supporting all that I do. You're one of a kind.

Chapter 1:
Self-Love Affirmations

I love myself and all that I'm created to be: my body, my skin, my hair and all that makes me uniquely me. No matter what society says, I have the right to be who I am.

I am proud of myself
and how far I've come.
I may not be where
I want to be, but
I've made the steps
necessary to improve
my life.

9

I forgive myself for accepting less at a time when I didn't know better. I know better now!

10

I will never give up on
who I am becoming.
The best is yet to
come for me.

I am enough. Always have been. Always will be. Screw anyone that thinks differently about me or attempts to get me to believe otherwise.

I am not my mistakes. They were lessons learned that have made me become a better woman.

13

I know good things will continue to happen in my life. I receive abundance because I know I'm deserving of it. I deserve a life of happiness with all the luxuries that I deem fit.

14

I love my strengths. I will not diminish them under any circumstances. I will nourish them at every opportunity.

I am whole and complete no matter who's in my life. I realize other people in my life merely compliment my existence. Me being complete is entirely my choice.

16

I will rise above the negativity that people will attempt to deflect on me. I won't give them that much control.

I uphold the standards that I set for myself. I will not reduce my value for anyone not willing to fit the bill.

I will not self-sabotage my happiness by refusing to heal.

I am forgiving myself, accepting myself, and releasing self-judgment. I recognize that I've been through a lot and it's okay.

I'm praying for the woman I'll be in 5+ years. I want her to be happy, loved, and living life unapologetically, doing what she loves.

21

My strength is not an opportunity to be taken advantage of; just because I can carry a lot, doesn't mean it's my job to pick it up.

I worked hard to become the woman I am growing to be, and I will never allow anyone to take my power away from me.

I will always remember to love myself on my worst days as I do on my best days. Self-love is a daily practice that I'm committed to in all aspects of my life.

It is safe to be me. I am free to express myself in whatever way I choose.

To speak my truth, to feel my truth, to know my truth, to be the truth is my authenticity. I'm fierce like that!

I will begin to shed the layers of what no longer serves me and begin to make room for new programming. I understand that I may have toxic traits that I have to fix within myself.

27

Chapter 2:
Mental Health Affirmations

I give myself permission to walk away from things that disrupt my peace and mental health.

29

I'm worth my own time, my own focus, and my own care. I have to be full in order for me to pour into others.

I understand
how I love myself
is how I teach
others to love me.

I'm proud of myself for how hard I'm trying. Each day is progress, no matter how small the steps are.

As I think about my priorities for the week ahead, I will ensure I'm near the top of the list.

Enforcing my boundaries doesn't make me a bad person. People who love me will respect them.

34

Getting divorced is okay. Ending toxic relationships is okay. Leaving a bad job is okay. Walking away from anything that leaves me unsettled and hurt is okay.

When things seem overwhelming for me, I will remember: one thought at a time, one task at a time, and one day at a time is all that it takes to push through.

To help better manage
my anxiety, I will focus
on things in which
I have control— my
words, my actions, my
body, and my spirit.

If it feels like too much, maybe it is too much. I will stop, rest, and reset when I need a break. My mental health matters. Burnout is not a badge of honor.

I realize that my mental health is just as important as my physical health. Understanding how my mind and body work together strengthens my ability to make positive choices.

39

I am most powerful when I'm my authentic self. When I leave her at home, I lose my power.

40

I don't have to wait for the world to approve me. I get the privilege of approving myself.

Every time something comes up that doesn't align with the real me, I'll be okay with letting it go. I'm not force-fitting anything in my life.

42

I choose to change my way of thinking, so I will not recycle my bad experiences. I will not create an inner environment of confusion— a state of feeling suffocated, unworthy, and unfree. That's not who I am.

43

I will not accept the notion of this is just how I am. This is the lie that we tell ourselves to stay comfortable in not being accountable for our own experiences.

I have the power
to change how
I feel in every
moment. I will
not be held
hostage by my
emotions.

45

I choose to forgive and let go of hurt because I'm bigger than my emotional scars.

I allow myself to be who I am without judgment. I give myself permission to grow and learn.

47

I give myself
permission to
do what is right
for me without
explanation.

48

Chapter 3:
Happiness Affirmations

It's okay for me to write a new story. The old one no longer exists. I'm committed to growing into the woman that I know I'm made to be.

I give myself permission to be gracious in the midst of hard times. I will extend myself the same grace that I give to others.

51

Being happy is a decision I've made today. I will not let others or temporary moments of dissatisfaction take that away from me.

52

I will move forward with a life that I'm excited to lead and adjust it accordingly. I have the right to make edits to my story.

53

Someday I will meet the happiest version of myself and that will be worth all the growing pains. Right now, I'm working on her.

What I want exists, and I won't settle until I get it. Period!

I understand that being happy is very personal and has nothing to do with anyone else. My happiness is completely on me.

56

My voice matters. I'm empowered to be authentically me.

When the going gets tough, I will think positive thoughts and radiate positive energy.

I possess everything I need to make positive changes in my life. It's on me to make the first step.

Today, I will make a conscious decision not to let anyone disrupt my vibe. My vibe is mine to own.

60

I don't chase, I attract. What belongs to me will find me.

61

When I'm my authentic self, my real gifts show up and show out on my behalf.

If I hide my true self by being someone I'm not, I'm hiding my purpose. I will make a conscious effort to be comfortable in my own skin and walk in my purpose.

63

When I look in the mirror, I will love what I see. I will love who I am. I'm committed to learning more about myself. I will unpack all the layers of inauthenticity that I use to make others feel comfortable.

64

I know who I am. I know what I want. I'm committed to show up to the world on my own terms.

65

I'm forgiving others to give myself peace. As I clear myself of judgments, forgiving others becomes easier.

66

I will come through this challenge with a better understanding of myself. Nothing is by chance.

Better days are ahead, and all things will work how and when they're supposed to. My time is mine and nothing can change that.

Today, I'm committed to ridding myself of complacency, baggage holding me down, and barriers in my way.

69

Chapter 4:
Relationship Affirmations

I will not tolerate relationships that hurt my soul out of the fear of loneliness. Screw that! I mean way more to myself than to allow that.

71

I will not disrespect myself by going back to someone that treated me with disrespect. I'll leave them where they had me, messed up!

72

I'm okay with waiting alone until I'm valued in the right way. I'd rather have a strong marriage than a messy divorce.

73

I attract only healthy relationships and have no room for toxic people.

74

I will only be in a loving relationship filled with unconditional love, respect, and trust. Those are all non-negotiable.

Today, is the last day of being hurt. I release the need to hold on to emotions tied to people who have wronged me. For me to move forward, I must take my power back.

76

I understand that every relationship starts within me. I am committed to self-love before loving someone else.

77

My relationships work out for the highest good of everyone involved.

78

I'm working on becoming the best version of myself. As a result, I am naturally becoming more confident and positive.

I will not let any past issues reflect on my current relationship. Lesson learned, but I will not recycle my experiences.

I am committed to staying true to myself in all my relationships. I will always draw healthy boundaries.

Today, I choose to communicate my emotions clearly so I can foster a healthy relationship. That toxic sh*t is dead!

I will not settle for less than I deserve out of fear of loneliness. I'm deserving of a healthy relationship that aligns with my heart's desires.

83

I am committed to be stress free in my relationship. I will be intentionally focused on my overall happiness.

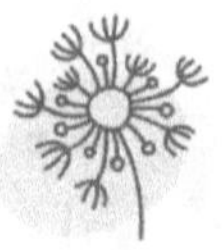

84

I will not allow society's standards of being a wife and a mom make me feel pressured to accept a relationship that's not meant for me. I will live life on my terms!

85

I will not apologize for refusing to be disrespected. Respect is a requirement of all my relationships and it's not up for debate!

86

I will never go against myself in any relationship. I will trust my better judgment of knowing when to walk away. I refuse to be mishandled.

87

The disrespect is all the closure I need. I'm not to be played with under any circumstances.

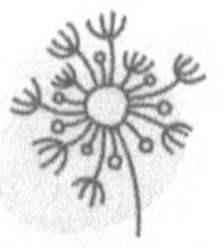

Chapter 5:
Abundance Affirmations

I was destined to be prosperous. I have abundance to share and to spare. I'm blessed like that.

I gratefully accept all the wealth and happiness that the creator sends to me every day.

91

My life flows effortlessly as doors of opportunity open to me everywhere, in every aspect of my life.

I am a magnet for wealth and abundance. I may not come from wealth, but I am committed to creating it.

I focus on the best in everything and everyone, and the best appears abundantly for me.

Abundance is around me; abundance is within me; abundance is throughout me.

95

My potential is unlimited! I am abundant! I am worthy and deserving of all things good!

I am in a state of fulfillment, have abundant love and joy in my life, and am free to do whatever I wish to do.

Abundance surrounds me. Today, I claim my share. I'm deserving of it.

Woman to Woman: Powerful Affirmations

The presence of joy in my heart releases abundance of good in my life.

99

I see right through hindrances and obstructions and know that abundance is all mine.

100

More good is waiting to reach me than I've ever experienced or imagined before.

101

I choose to live an abundant life. I know that's what I deserve.

I deserve the luxuries that life has to offer and will not let anyone make me feel bad for my standards.

103

I'm blessed, and I'm favored. I don't owe anyone an explanation. If they have a problem, they need to take it up with God.

Chapter 6:
Success Affirmation

I am prepared to take advantage of all the opportunities that are coming my way.

I make a difference in the world by simply existing in it. There is an opportunity with only my name on it.

I am a positive woman who attracts positive situations for success.

Woman to Woman: Powerful Affirmations

I deserve a seat at the table, even if I have to build my own.

I can accept criticism without taking it personally.

Each step in my career is helping me get to the end goal. I understand that I have to go through them to get there and that's okay.

111

I will find success
in all that I do
and keep growing
stronger everyday
so that nothing will
be able to pull me
down.

112

I'm committed to unlearn bad habits that interfere with my success.

Doors are opening for me. The wait wasn't punishment. It was preparation.

114

Better and bigger opportunities are in store for me. Blessings are headed my way!

115

I'm succeeding in my career even if I'm not where I want to be.

116

I'm worthy of the very best in life, and I allow myself to accept it.

117

Every career setback or roadblock helps me grow more as a person.

118

I have faith that everything will work out on my behalf because I'm doing my part.

119

My next season will be one of the best of my life. I'm attracting everything that I need to succeed.

Chapter 7:
Gratitude Affirmations

I am grateful for all the gifts that have been bestowed upon me.

I'm so grateful for all the little things that put a smile on my face.

123

Everything will happen to me suddenly, and I will be thankful I didn't give up. Blessings are coming.

124

I appreciate all people in my life, for each one brings an opportunity for learning to me. I now experience being fully supported by everyone in my life.

125

With my gratitude, I am close to the source of abundance.

The more I give thanks, the more things I have to be thankful for;
I am thankful for simply being alive today.

127

The more grateful I am, the more connected I am to the source and power of God.

128

Each day, I will immerse myself in gratitude and cultivate it as a habit.

Woman to Woman: Powerful Affirmations

Before going to sleep, I release all idle thoughts and focus on all my blessings. As I count my blessings, my blessings grow.

I am deeply and continuously grateful, and thereby I align to the outcomes of greatest blessings.

131

I am grateful for
all the miracles
God has to offer
me now and in the
future.

132

With the attitude of gratitude, I am able to move easily with life. With gratitude, I direct my energy according to my desires.

133

My life is full of so many things to be grateful for; every morning, I give thanks for another day of life. Seeing another day filled with opportunities is truly a blessing.

Woman to Woman: Powerful Affirmations

I am grateful to everyone who has helped me move closer to my goals. It's a blessing to have love and support.

135

I am immensely thankful for the power to change my life for the better.

Woman to Woman: Powerful Affirmations

I am grateful for all wealth and prosperity that flows into my life. I'm working towards manifesting the life that I envision for myself.

137

I gratefully accept all the wealth and happiness that the creator sends to me every day.

138

I am happy
and grateful for
everything I have
and receive daily.
I appreciate all; I
give thanks; I am
grateful.

I'm grateful for the experiences that have shaped me to become the woman I am today. I won't let the hard days win.

140

I am grateful for who I am. There is only one me in this world and that's amazing that God saw fit to mold me as He did.

Chapter 8:
Goal Setting Affirmations

I believe in myself and in my goals. Anything with my name attached to it will excel.

I am willing to step outside of my comfort zone to accomplish the goals I set for myself.

Woman to Woman: Powerful Affirmations

When I face blockers while working towards my goals; I'll move around them, over them, and through them.

Every day, I take steps to reach my goals because I'm committed to them.

My mind is clear, focused, and energized to accomplish all that I desire.

147

I will push my limits and will achieve great things. Nothing great comes easy.

I am focused on making my dreams a reality.

My goals fit perfectly with all areas of my life. Nothing is out of reach.

150

Defining my goals helps me to achieve my life's purpose.

151

Everything I do, supports the larger vision I have for my life.

152

Staying motivated and passionate about my dreams comes naturally because they are mine to achieve.

153

I devote time every day to research, study, plan, and implement my ideas that will help achieve my goals.

I release my fear of failing, and I express my creativity freely.

155

I'm committed to always making a total effort, even when the odds are against me. I won't allow fear to dictate anything that's attached to my name.

I won't let the hard days win. On the days that I lack motivation, my discipline will kick in.

Woman to Woman: Powerful Affirmations

Chapter 9:
Breaking Generational Curse Affirmations

I am not what happened to me. I am what I choose to become.

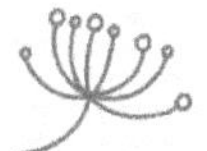

Whatever happens, my family will stay close. We will not be divided by unresolved hurt.

160

My children
will have a better
childhood than me.
I will always respect
them and allow
them to express
themselves.

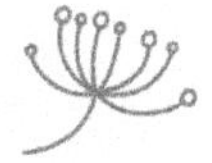

161

I will not allow my family history to control how I love myself, my children, or my spouse. I'm committed to breaking generational curses.

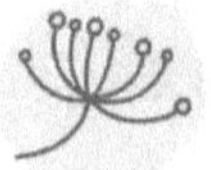

162

I will not tolerate lies, manipulation, chaos, drama, and disrespect just because someone is labeled as "family."

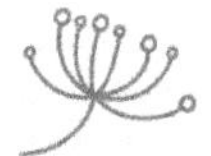

I will aim to be the woman I needed when I was younger. I am committed to healing so that I don't operate out of brokenness.

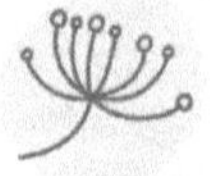

I refuse to let pain travel through my family lines. Family dysfunction will stop with me.

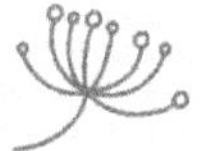

165

I'm dedicated to breaking the chain of pain patterns that have been passed down from previous generations.

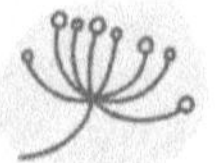

I will always have the strength to remove myself from a toxic environment and not live with it for the sake of family.

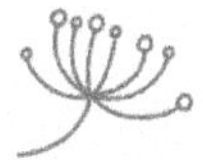

167

I'm keenly aware that it is easy to build up a healthy child than to repair a broken adult. I'm committed to raising my children in a loving and healthy environment.

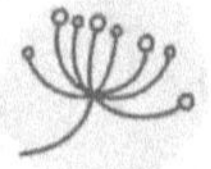

I accept that
not everyone
will be sorry or
understand how
they played a part
in my childhood
trauma.

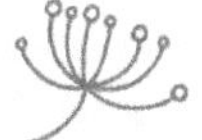

169

I'm slowly learning that some people aren't good for me, no matter how much I love them. Under these circumstances, I choose to love myself more and walk away.

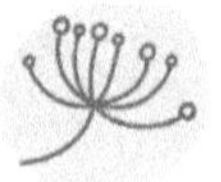

170

I will not become a prisoner of my past. I will be clear with myself that what happened to me doesn't define me.

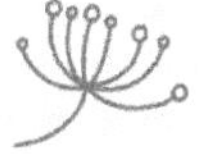

I refuse to inherit dysfunction and repeat what I lived through. I am better and will be better. I don't care who it offends.

172

I refuse to let the trauma I've experienced confine, define, or outshine me! I'm making a conscious effort to accept that I didn't deserve it and won't let it impact who I'll become.

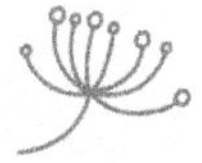

I'm committed to unlearning toxic behavior that was passed down from my parents. I won't put my children through the same thing.

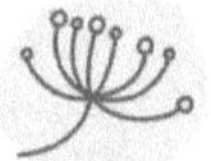

I am worthy of love, even if my parents didn't know how to love me. That was completely on them and had nothing to do with me.

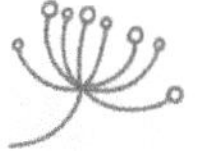

I will speak life, love, bravery, kindness, and hope over my children. I will break any generational curse off my family and me.

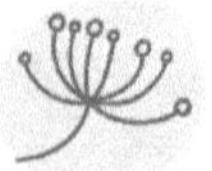

Woman to Woman: Powerful Affirmations

I forgive myself for tolerating things I shouldn't have when I didn't know how to love myself. I know better now and will never allow anyone to take that away from me.

177

I'm not them. They aren't me. There is power in my name, and I am committed to operating as my highest self and healing from trauma and hurt. I deserve all the greatness that life has to offer.

Printed in the USA
CPSIA information can be obtained
at www.ICGtesting.com
CBHW042325010124
3089CB00009B/559